Public Phenomena

by Temporary Services

with contributions by

Polonca Lovšin

Joseph Heathcott and Damon Rich

Boštjan Bugarič
Ana Čeligoj
Maša Cvetko
Marko Horvat
Meta Kos
Darjan Mihajlović
Danijel Modrej
Maja Modrijan
Sonja Zlobko

Half Letter Press LLC

Public Phenomena by Temporary Services

Published by:
Half Letter Press LLC
P.O. Box 12588
Chicago, IL 60612
USA
www.halfletterpress.com
publishers@halfletterpress.com

ISBN-13: 978-0-9818023-0-5
ISBN-10: 0-9818023-0-3

Edited and designed by Temporary Services
Cover images by Temporary Services

Temporary Services
P.O. Box 121012
Chicago, IL 60612
USA
www.temporaryservices.org
servers@temporaryservices.org

Printed in China by Permanent Printing Limited
www.permanent.com.hk

Temporary Services thanks the following people and organizations for their help and support for this book and our ongoing Public Phenomena project: AA Bronson, Krista Buecking, Jocelyn Davis, Julie Deamer & Outpost for Contemporary Art, Daniel Eatock, Anthony Elms and WhiteWalls, Ed Fella, Bonnie Fortune, Marc Herbst, Robert Herbst, Rob Kelly, Polonca Lovšin, Urša Jurman, Zoe Leonard, Multitudes, Nils Norman, Alexis Petroff, Tadej Pogacar and P74 Center and Gallery, Karel Pollack, Zena Sakowski, Persis Singh, Mike Smith at Mission Press, Linn Underhill, WHW (What, How, And For Whom), and Brian Whitener.

About the contributors:

Joseph Heathcott is a writer, curator, and educator living in New York, and is an associate professor of urban studies at The New School.

Polonca Lovšin is an artist and architect based in Skofja Loka, Slovenia. In her work, Lovšin focuses on everyday objects and inventions created with common sense and do-it-yourself methods. She is inspired by local knowledge and high technologies.

Damon Rich is an urban designer and founder of the Center for Urban Pedagogy (CUP). He lives and works in Newark, New Jersey.

The following people contributed images to the book:

Danijel Modrej and Darjan Mihajlović (pp. 29, top; 31, top; 80-81; 104; 140), Sonja Zlobko and Marko Horvat (pp. 31, top; 139, top right), Maša Cvetko (p. 105); Polonca Lovšin (pp. 64-71; 106-107), Archive of the National Training and Information Center (p. 88), Boštjan Bugarič (p. 138), Ana Čeligoj (p. 139, top left), Meta Kos (p. 139, bottom), Maša Cvetko (p. 141, top), Maja Modrijan (p. 141, bottom), Alexis Petroff (p. 146, top), and Zoe Leonard (p. 146, bottom, originally published by Steidl & Fotomuseum Winterthur)

Front cover: Makeshift Barriers – Urbana, Temporary Services, 2008
Back cover: Ghost Houses – Chicago, Temporary Services, 2006

This publication was made possible by grants from Art Matters, CEC Artslink, and support from P.A.R.A.S.I.T.E. Institute.

art matters

 CECartslink

P.A.R.A.S.I.T.E. Institute

Dedicated to all of the uncredited modifiers, inventors, communicators, and public citizens whose work has changed our common landscape.

CONTENTS

PUBLIC PHENOMENA: AN INTRODUCTION
By Temporary Services

When we step outside our homes, we enter what is called "public space." We don't often give much thought to what public space actually is. How is it formed? How could it be different?

Public space is a confusing term that is often used in error. The spaces we move through, share with others, and think of as public are usually privately owned, heavily regulated, or controlled by government or corporate interests. We find that this is increasingly so in American cities, in this era where fear-driven assessment rather than people-centered rationality guides how space is controlled and strangers interact. This drastically limits how we use and think about these spaces.

The city we know best is Chicago. Like many cities around the world, Chicago is covered in surveillance cameras. We are encouraged to treat all situations as potentially dangerous, all strangers as criminals. This keeps us divided and makes us easier to control. In our highly regulated urban landscape, one has to search to find the little cracks in public space, or shared spaces as we prefer to call them, where citizens have taken the opportunity to insert new creative possibilities or try out new ways of being in their cities. Uses of these shared spaces are often nuanced, contradictory, and full of just barely tapped possibilities. The small punctures that people make in their cities sometimes point to the more liberatory, directly democratic ideas of public space that we long for – spaces where people are empowered to act, change their societies and meet face to face with strangers who differ from them.

The essays and photographs in this book document unofficial, informal modifications and uses of the shared spaces of cities. These are publicly visible instances of displacement, movement, installation, and change that are not expected or usually tolerated as normal behavior. People constantly manipulate their environment to suit their needs. Activities that take place on private property but are publicly visible, such as a makeshift barrier, help to generate an environment of possibility. People who see these "private" modifications often mimic the same activity in their own publicly visible spaces. The actions we call "public phenomena" are often initiated by individuals or small groups, but can sometimes be practiced citywide by thousands of people. Through conscious or unconscious repetitions of these actions, patterns form and become visible through their amalgamation. It is through seeing phenomena, and recognizing it as an unofficial change to a space or structure, that a heightened awareness of personal civic desires can emerge.

Awareness of public phenomena comes from a habitual experience of a specific place. The photos in this book try to capture this experience and share it.

We intend for this book to be both a research tool and a guide to visualizing a different way of defining the landscape of cities. This book is not a substitute for the deep, intuitive sense of place that one gets every day just from inhabiting and moving through cities.

We intentionally try to document things in an accessible, non-academic manner. We are more interested in the generative nature of what we study rather than having a mastery over a discourse, or aiding professionals to design our cities "better." This book is not intended to be a manual for urban planners or architects. It celebrates the opposite impulses of those pursuits. We are interested in opening things up and finding cracks, not absorbing or fetishizing informal activities. The research we do is something that others can easily join in or develop on their own in ways that are directly analogous to the creation of public phenomena.

This doesn't mean that it is impossible to do extensive research into the reasons things are changed, or the history of such behavior. We encourage this and have provided a couple of examples in this book. Polonca Lovšin visits a man in Ljubljana who has filled his yard with signs, gadgets, statues, and a range of other things to communicate with his neighbors and passersby. A short essay by Joseph Heathcott and Damon Rich gives an introduction to signs made by block clubs in Chicago and why they exist. These signs were one of the first things that Temporary Services started to document many years ago.

We collect enough images for patterns to become visible. We can't possibly re-cord every example in a city, nor is this necessary. We take photos while traveling away from home. Some themes become clear immediately. Others take years to present themselves as something worthy of sustained investigation. We have many additional thematic collections in process, but these lack enough examples to demonstrate a behavioral pattern.

We show multiple instances of a single phenomena, presented together with other phenomena. Too often artists treat similar subjects as an isolated aesthetic experience in a single photograph with a nice frame. We are not interested in making a commodity or a set of single iconic images, but rather a tool for understanding the world around us.

There are always things that are too hard to photograph, or manage to appear only when we don't have a camera. Some behaviors are seasonal and can only be captured during particular instances, as with Parking Place Savers during snowstorms in Chicago. Other activities are relegated to particular neighborhoods and are easily overlooked if one is not moving through specific parts of a town.

While our photos tend to favor a clear, crisply focused and well-centered approach to documentation, the poetics of much of what we take photos of are not lost on us. We find much amusement and many serendipitous or absurd moments in cities. We hope that people can also experience some of that pleasure in the actions we document.

People continuously work against the design of the products they buy and the houses they live in. The city planning they inherit is usually decided long before they moved to their neighborhood. People naturally move against all kinds of control. There is evidence of this all over the world and in the wide range of activities covered in this book. If people's needs are not met by the infrastructure of their city, neighborhood, or block, people will adjust their surroundings to their needs.

Temporary Services strives to conduct visual research that opens up new possibilities for how the spaces of our cities can be thought about and used. Most cities are dominated by the interests of capital, business, and indifferent, inaccessible, public bureaucracy that limits the possible uses of public space. This myopic vision for our shared spaces results in a really boring situation for both experiencing cities, as well as making art in public. This seemingly leaves artists with two options: you can either make official public art (with permission from your government, permits, lots of money, sponsorships from business, and the other accoutrements of being "public artists") or you can take an interventionist approach (which all but guarantees limited exposure, minor impact, and a lack of sustained resistance to unnecessary, oppressive norms).

Public phenomena can include long-term modifications that become the norm, outside of permission from authorities. People respect things like informal street memorials and let them continue for years even though they might have been illegal to install. Other phenomena may last for as short as several days or hours. It is exciting to have a city in flux with lots of ephemeral changes from the bottom. We prefer this over having decisions handed down to us from up top that we have to live with for decades. In our creative practice, which has often included doing projects on the street, we have been concerned with what we can do — on our own or with others — on a small and manageable scale without wading through endless city bureaucracy. We like testing out what is possible and react positively to a lot of the gestures we document in our Public Phenomena photos.

The instigators of these modifications were similarly willing to create the changes that they needed to see in direct, everyday ways. As our group's name suggests, we appreciate gestures that are often temporary in their nature. Cities should be much more flexible than they are, and fully reflect the diverse needs of their inhabitants. Part of that flexibility could include developing public art projects that don't last forever. These could be projects that don't require extremely expensive maintenance budgets that go on for decade upon decade. We don't have the egos for that kind of work and don't seek out opportunities to do things that will be imposed upon city residents forever.

If cities allowed a broader range of ways of being, working, and doing things in public space without fear of legal repercussions at every turn, this would help open up art practice more than anything else. Allowing more informal modifications to happen on individual and neighborhood levels could eventually make things like public art programs unnecessary. One finds humor, irregularity, wonder, confusion, mystery and the confrontation with someone's unregulated and uncensored passion in the kinds of things documented in this book. Often these expressions are not explicitly or intentionally political in their execution, but they commonly fly in the face of the encouraged, legal, or demanded civic solution to a particular problem. Likewise, they are often not explicitly artistic, yet these actions commonly reveal a similar concern with form, materials, and creative, highly economical, or sensitive uses of space.

Artists have a vital role in making sense of city life and how shared spaces are used in urban and rural settings. There is a long, well established tradition of looking at and making art about cities in the ways that this book does. These efforts present an understanding of how a city's uses are visually communicated to visitors and inhabitants alike. A resource section at the end of the book presents others' attempts to understand how cities function. These books, art projects, and web-based archives have informed Public Phenomena over the years.

Artists' personal practices have also moved well beyond the formal, conservative constraints of notions like "site specificity" (making art for a specific site where the content and form reflect that site's history, use, people, etc.) to practices that interrogate what city spaces are for, how they are used, and how they can be opened up to greater possibility and experimentation.

Temporary Services has been documenting, sharing, and talking about Public Phenomena since we started working together. This is the nexus of human creativity. When something needs to happen, humans make it happen, despite the circumstance. Whether it's a list of demands for our fellow humans (Block Club Signs), an assertion of our own personal presence in the world (Parking Place Savers), absurd attempts to reign in nature (Cropped and Fence-Eating Trees) or allowing markers of what we had long ago to remain (Ghost Houses), our collective footprint chooses a myriad of ways to grind against the surface.

ABOUT TEMPORARY SERVICES

Temporary Services is Brett Bloom, Salem Collo-Julin and Marc Fischer. We are based in Illinois and have existed, with several changes in membership and structure, since 1998. We produce exhibitions, events, projects, and publications. The distinction between art practice and other creative human endeavors is irrelevant to us.

Temporary Services started as an experimental exhibition space in a working class neighborhood of Chicago. Our name directly reflects the desire to provide art as a service to others. It is a way for us to pay attention to the social context in which art is produced and received. Having "Temporary Services" displayed on our window helped us to blend in with the cheap restaurants, dollar stores, currency exchanges, and temporary employment agencies on our street. We were not immediately recognizable as an art space. This was partly to stave off the stereotypical role we might have played in the gentrification of our neighborhood. We were not interested in selling art or making objects to be commodified.

Experiencing art in the places we inhabit on a daily basis remains a critical concern for us. It helps us move art from a privileged experience to one more directly related to how we live our lives. A variety of people should decide how art is seen and interpreted, rather than continuing to strictly rely on those in power. We move in and out of officially sanctioned spaces for art, keeping one foot in the underground the other in the institution. Staying too long in one or the other isn't healthy. We are interested in art that takes engaging and empowering forms. We collaborate amongst ourselves and with others, even though this may destabilize how people understand our work.

Temporary Services seeks to create and participate in ethical relationships that are not competitive and are mutually beneficial. We develop strategies for harnessing the ideas and energies of people who may have never participated in an art project before, or who may feel excluded from the art community. We mobilize the generosity of many people to produce projects on a scale that none of us could achieve in isolation. We strive towards aesthetic experiences built upon trust and unlimited experimentation.

PARKING PLACE SAVERS – Chicago, Mexico City, Athens, Ljubljana

In any densely populated city people compete for access to space for housing, recreation, work, and parking. Between heavy traffic and constant roadwork, there are already large strains and stresses on people who drive in Chicago under normal conditions; when it snows heavily things get even tenser. Public transportation doesn't provide the best means of getting around for everyone. Some parts of the city are only accessible after a couple hours of riding on buses and trains. Parking – already scarce in many neighborhoods in normal weather – becomes a great point of contestation after a heavy snowstorm. After a person spends an hour digging his car out from under the snow, he often feels entitled to that space and lays claim with a makeshift parking place saver made from whatever materials are on hand. This practice happens all over Chicago and isn't specific to any group of people or given neighborhood. People are often afraid to take another person's parking place because of fears of violence to their person or vandalism to their car. Even the current mayor of Chicago has encouraged people to respect each other's place savers despite the illegality of this practice. We often joke that after a snowstorm the streets resemble a grassroots Arte Povera or Minimalist sculpture festival. This practice has also helped us to find some nice chairs once the snow melts. These photos were taken in 2007.

Parking Place Savers – Chicago

In addition to people and cars, many of the streets of Mexico City, Mexico, are jammed with vendors. Booths, stands, tables, and blankets display everything from food to bootleg CDs, DVDs, hernia belts, and boxing gloves. The booths clog space normally allotted for parking on both sides of many streets. This leaves only a single cramped lane for cars to pass down the center, and little if any space to park during peak vending hours. Not surprisingly, many parking place savers are created from remnants of the retail world such as long cardboard tubes that were originally used for bolts of fabric. These photos were taken in 2007.

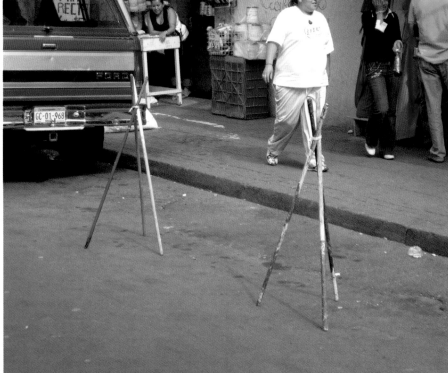

Athens, Greece is a bustling city of approximately 3.8 million people. It has the highest per capita car ownership in the European Union with nearly 2 million vehicles. There are not enough parking spaces for all of them. Many homemade parking place savers can be observed throughout the city – particularly in areas where the streets are older and narrower. These photos were taken in 2007.

ΓΚΑΡΑΖ
ΛΕΙΤΟΥΡΓΕΙ 24 ΩΡΕΣ

Ljubljana, the capital of Slovenia, is a small city nestled between the Alps and the Adriatic Sea. Its geography gives it a compact quality that makes Ljubljana feel very urban despite its population of less than 300,000 people. After leaving Yugoslavia in 1991, Slovenia developed its own car culture and the car became a sought-after status symbol. Slovenia is the wealthiest of the former Yugoslavian states. As Ljubljana's prosperity increased people bought more vehicles, exacerbating pre-existing automobile-related problems. There are many cars, but the city was not planned with enough street parking to accommodate all of them. Additionally, nearly 100,000 people commute into the city from outlying areas every day. This creates a lot of competition for parking. People tend to park in bike lanes, on sidewalks, and very close to houses – wherever they can find or make parking. One can see a variety of efforts where long wooden poles are leaned against buildings to save parking spots very close to houses, or to prevent others from parking there at all. These photos were taken in 2007.

PREPOVEDANO
USTAVLJANJE
IN PARKIRANJE
NA DOVOZU,
REZERVIRANO ZA STRANKE

HANDMADE "NO PARKING" SIGNS – Ljubljana

The parking place savers in the previous section are one-way people claim public spaces for their cars. These handmade "no parking" signs, which often threaten people with having their vehicles towed, are a two-dimensional attempt to deter people from occupying or blocking private space. These photos were taken in 2007.

MOTORCYCLE LOCKS – Athens

Walking in some sections of Athens is like playing Russian roulette in streets loaded with motorized vehicles. In addition to cars, there are many motorcycles and scooters on the streets of Athens – all seemingly driving in their own in-between, made-up lanes. Consequently, there are tons of motorcycle locks to accompany the vehicles. All over the city, people leave the locks as placeholders for their motorcycles. One lock, shown in the bottom right corner on the next page, had grown into a tree and seemed to still be in use. These photos were taken in 2007.

LOCKED – Mexico City

Shops in Mexico City are locked down so heavily that the vast rows of padlocks become a striking visual detail in the early morning and evening hours when the stores are closed. In addition to roll-down walls of metal with heavily padlocked doors, many retailers use an additional succession of locks to secure their metal roll-down doors to anchors that are lodged into gouged-out sidewalks. These photos were taken in 2007.

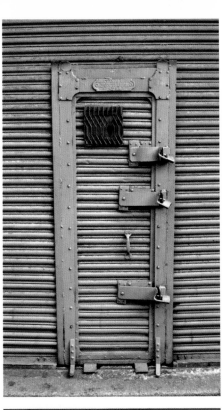

Locked – Mexico City **47**

PLANT PROTECTORS – Mexico City, Mumbai

In Mexico City and Mumbai, India, two of the world's most densely packed cities, a range of different metal protective devices are employed along sidewalks to prevent potted plants and trees from being stolen by petty thieves, damaged by cars that could easily back into them on crowded streets, and to keep the planters from being used as places to rest. These photos were taken in Mexico City in 2007, and in Mumbai in 2008.

MAKESHIFT BARRIERS – Chicago, Ljubljana, Urbana

Fences, boards, plastic, and cords. We've seen a lot of different self-made solutions for keeping the public out of private spaces. Owing a bit to the sometimes urgent need to create a barrier, and a lot to human ingenuity, the makeshift barriers in these photographs shine a light on the unintentional (or sometimes very intentional) public face that people create for their property boundaries. Many of these photos show quick fixes, or stop-gap measures to alter an existing "professional" fence that is falling apart or does not extend as far as is needed. Some of the barriers are clearly put in place to add a secondary or even tertiary layer of security against people, the elements, animals, or all of the above. Buildings in Chicago that are structurally compromised, in disuse, or in transition, usually do not remain accessible; they are almost always barricaded with wood sheeting. Professional companies race to the scene of fires in competition to be the first ones hired to do the boarding up. Many of these barriers over the windows and entries of disused or damaged buildings look distinctly homemade. They are often the work of property owners or residents who weren't able to afford to have the pros cover their windows or doorways for them, or repair or extend their fencing. The resulting effect is a more visually dissonant patchwork of scraps – something inventive, funky, ad hoc and poignant that we find refreshing in a sea of banal, perfect, stylistically continuous solutions to everyday problems. These photos were taken between 2005 and 2007.

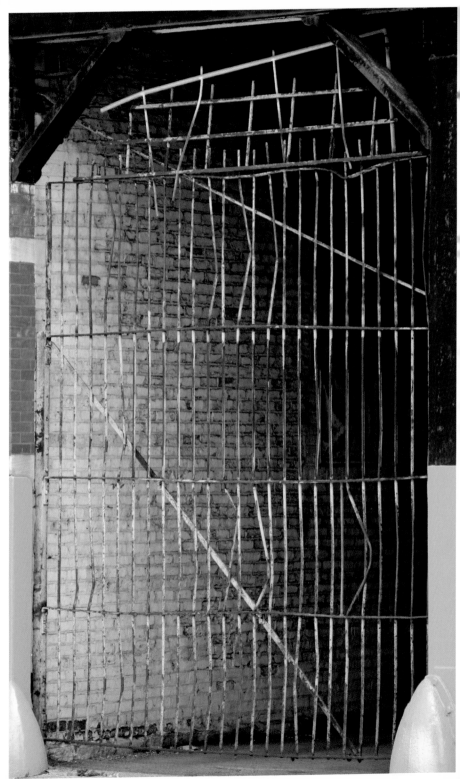

60 Makeshift Barriers – Chicago

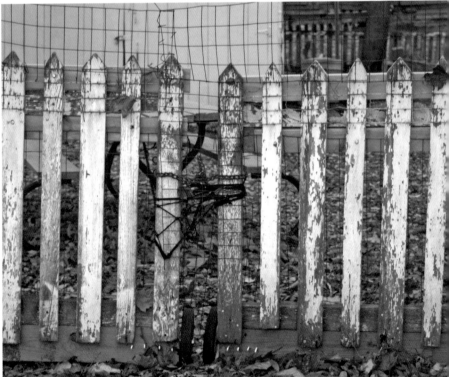

THE INVENTORY OF MR. ROVEN'S GARDEN
by Polonca Lovšin

Heavy traffic runs on Celovška, the main road leading from the center of Ljubljana to the north of the city. During peak hours, many locals take the road parallel to Celovška to the suburb of Poljane, and drive with high speed to their homes. This is the main reason why Mr. Roven, who lives on this road, overloaded his garden with all kinds of metal sheets and signs for slower speeds, including ones that function like propellers. Mr. Roven is retired and diabetic. He has trouble walking and standing on his legs. He has arranged his chaotic and mechanical garden so he can enjoy the view from his kitchen window where he spends his days looking out. Wind turbines and bicycles are on poles. Other things arranged in the garden are constructed out of found and waste material. Many of them have an aesthetic reason, to make his view through the window attractive, but some of them are also to make his life easier. I talked to Mr. Roven about his garden on December 10, 2007, and took these pictures.

Polonca Lovšin: When did you start arranging your garden in the way it is now?

Mr. Roven: After my mother's death. She would never allow me to do this. Even when she was not healthy, she had her garden always in order. There were no

weeds and the earth was broken up. I cannot sustain the garden in this way any-more because I have troubles to lean and that is why I stopped growing vegetables. My mother died nine years ago and after that the garden stayed empty and aban-doned. I have collected metal, objects and stuff people would throw away behind the railway. I collected all that, among them many old bicycles, and sheltered them in the garden. I was thinking to myself that these items might be useful sometime in the future. I observed the bearings of a steering wheel and the poles of the fence that were lying there, and came up with the idea of windmills of all kinds. I even used whole bicycles as windmills.

I have done all this work in a sitting position in front of my kitchen window. Now I have hired a man who is taking care of the house and garden. He is coming from Banja Luka but I call him Balkanec – the inhabitant of the Balkans. He is coming from a peasant family but has trained himself to work with metal. He was working for a boss who demanded very precise work and that is why he is precise too. I have given the ideas and he realized them and installed them in my garden.

Gondola

This invention helps me get my mail from the mailbox without walking. I have seen Italians in Naples that use a rope hanging down from a window with a basket at-tached to the end. They put newspapers and small things in the basket and pull them up. My gondola is done out of a fishing pole that is attached to my kitchen window and with thin wire connected with the open mailbox. In the past I was fishing and I have seen the pole lying around the house and thought to use it. [See top two images on page 68.]

Catwalk

The catwalk is a simple wooden board with crossbars connecting the kitchen window and the ground. My fifteen-year-old cat uses it to go in and out. [See the bottom image on page 68.]

Moving sculptures

There are aluminum plates and windmills fixed on the ends of poles. The bearings from steering wheels make them move. I like them because they remind me of trees. [See top two images on page 69.]

Traffic signs

There are signs that remind people of the speed limit, dangers on the road, kids on the road, old woman on the road, handicapped people, and reflectors. I have writ-ten the big one, on the old satellite dish, in a hope it will not be possible to ignore it. But my hope was for nothing. They hit me once when I was going out and my collarbone was broken and my shoulder sprained. This is all because people drive too fast. [See bottom two images on page 69.]

Stick with keys

A snap-link was welded to the end of an old ski pole. I hang the master key on the snap-link and hand the pole through the kitchen window to visitors. I found the ski pole behind the railroad tracks. People threw them away. I picked it up, and Balkanec welded them together.

Children's bicycle on a pole

There was an accident in front of my house and this happened because of this traffic. A young boy around the age of 10, I assume, was coming up this side road. A fast car coming on this main road hit him. Fortunately there was nothing serious, the boy was only frightened and scared. The driver was happy that nothing was wrong with the boy and offered him a huge chocolate. In the first moment the boy was afraid to take it, but then he took it and started running like hell in the direction of the railroad tracks. He left his bicycle behind him and never returned to pick it up. The bicycle was lying there distorted for some time. After a while I fixed it and suggested to Balkanec to make this sculpture. We added a sign, "Child on the road" that is written on the plate and is rotating in the wind. [See top left image on page 71.]

The tree stump with the roof

This was a nut tree, which I decided to cut down because I only had expenses with it. I had to hire a gardener each year to cut down the branches. Now it is a stump around one meter high and we added a triangular roof that is to protect the Jesus on the cross I have fixed on the stump. But in all honesty, this roof has no practical function because Jesus is made of aluminum. [See top right image on page 71.]

Aluminum saints, bugs and similar things

In the past years I have found a lot of aluminum lying behind the railroad tracks. Nowadays it is hard to find it. Aluminum is expensive and some people are collecting it. There used to be a workshop of the Agroservis factory from Koseze nearby. They were casting aluminum cuffs for firemen's uniforms. I knew the general manager well and he has used the leftovers of hot aluminum to cast old-fashioned irons, sacred figures like Jesus and saints, bugs and similar things. These were leftovers for him and he didn't make business with them. Throughout the years he accumulated many pieces. We would drink a glass of wine together from time to time and he offered me these figures. He didn't want to melt them once again and use the material for something else since he has already put some time into them. I agreed to take them. You can see the eternal flame, a bug on the garage, and many Jesus figures placed around the garden. [See bottom left image on page 71.]

Fountain

A small fountain was placed under the kitchen window so that I can hear the sound of water. A small barrel for wine was placed in a higher position and filled with water. It has a plastic tube running through the head and into the mouth of

the Lion sculpture. Water runs out of its mouth and drops into a used bathtub. Everything is made out of reused and found materials. [See bottom right image on page 71.]

Rooster
There was a craftsman's shop for copper near the Ljubljanica river. The man was doing roosters for people's roofs. It is a tradition in Slovenia to put them on the roof. We believe they protect the inhabitants of the house against fire and lightning. This one works perfectly and by that I know what kind of weather there will be the next day. I have fixed it on the pole and even though it is small you will not believe it took a big sheet of copper for that. [See top right image on page 69.]

Dwarves and lions
I bought these in a shopping mall because they were on sale. Dwarves are holding lamps powered by solar cells, but they are not working well. My horoscope sign is Leo and that is why I have taken the lions too. [See below.]

Flags and Christmas lights
I have a flag holder fixed in the window frame in the upper floor. But since I can not walk upstairs, I never put a flag there. I also have Christmas lighting arranged in a way so I can turn it off or on only by pressing one button; I don't even need to stand up.

ANTENNAS – Zagreb

Antennas and satellite dishes cover the roofs of many buildings in Zagreb, Croatia. The sheer quantity of these devices throughout the city is astounding. The wiring and attachments aren't integrated into the infrastructures of the buildings, but dangle precariously off the sides of structures creating possible interference with other devices, as well as extending the presence of the entire operation. The rooftops of Zagreb seem to be covered by invasive gardens of metal plants, a veritable communications-topiary that starts to resemble small tree branches, or even human arms and fingers, reaching out for clarity.

CROPPED AND FENCE-EATING TREES – Chicago

While human life carries on around them, trees in urban areas quietly but forcefully grow in unexpected ways that property owners may not notice until they have become severe. We have seen many examples of trees that have "eaten" fences – growing over the metal, absorbing it and thriving for years undeterred by human interventions. More attentive and less tolerant property owners will notice this behavior and aggressively crop the trees – further calling attention to what these plants were doing when no one was looking. These photos were taken between 2005 and 2007.

Cropped and Fence-Eating Trees – Chicago

BASKETBALL HOOPS – Chicago

Homemade Basketball hoops are often an indication of city spaces that lack adequate or safe parks and recreational outlets for children. In Chicago, where one can also spot store-bought hoops and backboards, the most common no-budget alternative is a scrap of wood and a scavenged plastic milk delivery crate with its bottom ripped out. The support surface for these hoops is usually a tree along the street or a telephone pole in Chicago's alleys. The backboard with a destroyed or missing "net" is just as common a sight as the functional basketball hoop – a likely victim of too many slam dunks. These photos were taken between 2005 and 2007.

BLOCK SIGNS

by Joseph Heathcott and Damon Rich
with passages by Shell Trap

If you could change one thing in this neighborhood, what would you change? If you had a magic button you could push that fixed something, what would it say on that button? That would be my pitch. You had to push, because most people had never been asked that question. They'd been told what was wrong, but they'd never been asked.
– Shell Trap, National Training and Information Center, interviewed May 2007

When you first see a typical Chicago block club sign you might think it rather bossy. The sign is an injunction, severe in tone:

NO DRUG SELLING. NO GAMBLING. NO DOGS UNLEASHED. NO AUTO REPAIRS.

While this list of prohibitions might pass in wealthier neighborhoods as unspoken norms of everyday life, they take on urgent meaning wherever the block clubs commit them to signage. Decades of neglect by civil authorities leave these working class and poor neighborhoods to bear the brunt of drug dealing, vandalism, dog fighting, stray animals, and rackets in gambling, prostitution, and auto parts fencing.

The signs point to the hope for a different kind of neighborhood – one that most Americans take for granted. Working with spray cans, fat permanent markers, sticky vinyl letters, and stencils on wood and metal, the sign makers translate communal frustrations for wide public consumption. Sometimes simple, sometimes elaborate, the block club signs artfully capture the blunt force of frank Chicago speech.

Staked into the ground at the end of each block, the signs seem to burst forth from the spontaneous will of an organic community. But this is not the case. Chicago's block club signs result from a deliberate and organized social movement, and they reflect a distinctively American style of civic action. As material culture and every-day art practice, they emerge directly from the contentious, rambunctious, messy, and democratic tradition of Chicago-style community organizing.

In the late 1930s, the Chicago Area Project, an anti-youth delinquency nonprofit run by sociologist Clifford Shaw, tapped the talented young criminologist Saul Alin-sky to start a program in the "Back of the Yards" – the industrial neighborhood featured in Upton Sinclair's *The Jungle*. Eventually, Alinsky decided that his work was merely tinkering in the margins of giant social problems instead of making signifi-cant change. To find more effective ways to organize disempowered urban com-munities, he began to compile tactics from older social movements like the Con-gress of Industrial Organizations and the Communist Party of the United States of America. Slowly, Alinsky found ways to apply the techniques developed by unions to organize communities.

Through the Industrial Areas Foundation (IAF), founded in 1940, Alinsky and his trainees worked by identifying key players and power holders in communities, and then building consensus among churches, unions, and civic groups to directly challenge the authority of municipal agencies and politicians. The coalitions of in-stitutions would pursue small wins – demands that were met – on a steady basis to build their power and make the changes they wanted to see. The successes enjoyed by workers through unions could now spread beyond the factory and into the world of urban politics.

The Alinskyite model took shape in the crucible of the modern industrial city, with working-class constituencies already primed by first or second-hand experience with unionization. The Industrial Areas Foundation functioned much like a central labor council, drawing its representatives from different institutions to service on the governing body: priests, rabbis, deacons, union bosses, and civic club officers. The presence of these institutions meant that Alinsky and his lieutenants could quickly identify and tap key players in a community, and rapidly mobilize support for the IAF and the constituents they served.

After World War II, these mass institutions and the civic culture they supported eroded significantly. Industries downsized and relocated to low-wage regions outside of cities, eliminating high-paying industrial jobs. At the same time, older White ethnic groups left the city in growing numbers, pulled to the suburbs by shifting job markets, and pushed by racial panic upon the arrival of African-Americans from the South. Panic-peddlers and blockbusters inflamed these fears to accelerate property turnover, loosen markets, and increase profits. As people moved, the institutions that catered to them changed. Without the mass institutions that once provided the IAF with their power base, community organizers found themselves operating in a more atomized culture, needing new methods to organize people power.

The National Training and Information Center is one organization that has built on the Alinskyite tradition while adjusting it to the realities of contemporary American cities. NTIC organizers start by knocking on doors, talking with people, and helping them to talk to one another. When people in a neighborhood talk, they share stories and commiserate over common frustrations. Hot-button issues emerge quickly.

So usually when I'd hit a block, I'd walk up and down through the alleys, looking for a pile of trash or a pothole or a bad building or an abandoned car. Because most of the time when you ask that question, people say, "Oh it's a nice neighborhood, no problems." So I'd say, well, I'd lie and say, "Your neighbor mentioned that pothole at the end of the block," and they'd say, "Oh yeah! I always tear up my tire. That is pretty bad."

Organizers work with local residents, coaching them, role-playing, and building their confidence to run a meeting. The enabling works both ways: the organizer gains legitimacy by knocking on doors in the company of a recognized community member. The community member develops leadership capacity and rallies people around issues of concern to them. This process of organizing builds the neighborhood's capacity to solve problems; in the process, organizers leave behind a stronger neighborhood with community leaders that live there.

When organizers begin their work in a community, the problems are small. Organizers call these "winnable issues," demands that can usually be met by holding negligent municipal agencies accountable for things like rat abatement and filling potholes. Small initial victories fuel the future success of the organization, and the organizer works hard to deliver them while taking care to let residents lead meetings and accountability sessions with city officials and landlords. The organizer facilitates by providing information, strategies, and ideas on running meetings and getting people out to participate.

My first boss sent me to Austin because he thought maybe I could take the block clubs in the area to the next level, which we called civic groups. Basically Chicago is laid out on a grid, every four blocks you have a major street, and out of those eight square blocks between the major streets, we formed civic groups that could take on bigger issues like slum buildings in the area. The idea of a block club is to find good leaders you can kick up to the next level of the civic group, where you can take on bigger issues, and have the power of 200 or 300 people.

By knocking on doors and pulling people together, NTIC builds neighborhood organizations literally from the ground up, starting with the basic urban unit of the block. With time and hard work, block clubs combine into civic clubs, civic clubs form neighborhood organizations, and these in turn coalesce into larger city-wide federations. The glue that holds it all together is the meeting – the face-to-face interactions where residents argue, deliberate, consent and dissent in true grass-roots democratic form.

We were crazy on block clubs. My turf was the railroad tracks on the east, Lake Street on the north, the expressway on the south, and Austin Avenue on the west. I had 48 block clubs that met every month, 12 street clubs, which were four blocks in a row that met every month, and I had three civics that met once a month. I went to all these meetings. I had block club meetings Monday to Friday nights. If a block club met on Saturday night, I said I wouldn't come.

By combining the power and bodies of individual blocks, groups build their ability to make demands of city and state governments – and ultimately courts, federal agencies, and Congress. The block sign signals the beginning of this community power, phase one for a collectively controlled living environment. The history of the block sign shows that collective power requires a patiently built and locally based social structure for its exercise, and that the process of building and nurturing this structure can be taught and disseminated. The serial aesthetic of the block sign, unity in difference, springs from this each-one-teach-one mode of transmission.

So next time you're walking down Austin Avenue and come upon a block sign, don't take offense at the NO! You've got to read that list of prohibitions as the terms of a temporary truce in a larger struggle, a public agreement in service of larger goals. Ultimately, whenever you see a block sign, you are looking at a community that hopes one day to have no need for that sign.

RESPECT OUR HOMES. HAVE A NICE DAY. GOD BLESS YOU.

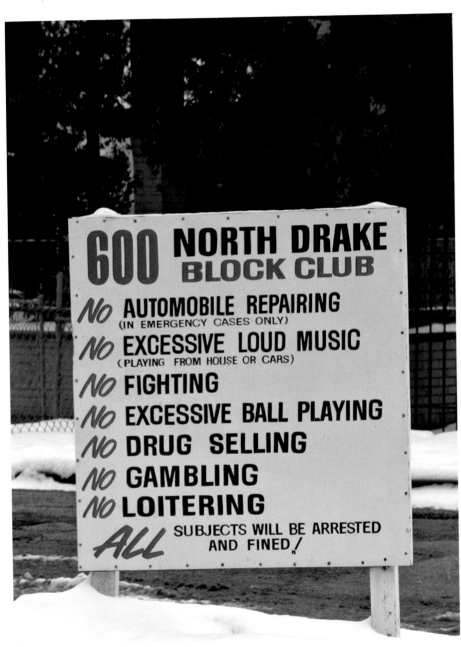

300 AKE LOC
RULES

NO DRUG SELLING
NO GAMBLING
NO LITTERING   STAY
NO CAR REPAIRS   OUT
NO CAR WASHING   OF MY
NO LOUD MUSIC   GRASS
PLEASE COVER YOUR
     ALCOHOL

     CAPS

WELCOME
700 N Christiana
Block Club
Please Drive Slow:
NO
1. Loitering or Littering
2. Ball Playing
3. Car Repairing
4. Car Washing (Alley's Only)
5. Disabled Vehicles
6. Parking on Lawn
7. Playing on Lawn
8. Drinking on Street
9. Honking Car Horns
10. Motor Cycles on Sidewalk

WELCOME TO
WE ARE OUR BROTHER'S KEEPER
800 & 900 N. TRUMBULL AVE
BLOCK CLUB

NO DRUG SELLING
   LOUD MUSIC
NO CAR REPAIRING
   LOITERING
NO LITTERING
   GAMBLING
   DRINKING ALCOHOL

COMMUNITY POLICING WATCH &
RKS WITHCAPS POLICE

WELCOME
500 N. AVERS
BLOCK CLUB

NO DRUGS
CAR WASHING
SOLICITING
LITTERING
NO LOUD MUSIC
CAR REPAIRING
SPEEDING
GAMBLING
NO LOITERING
BALL PLAYING FRONT

WE WILL CALL THE POLICE
IF ANYONE IS FOUND IN VIOLATION

WELCOME
700 N. ST. LOUIS
BLOCK CLUB

NO DRUG ACTIVITY
LOITERING
CAR WASHING IN FRONT
NO BALL PLAYING IN FRONT
SOLICITING OR GANG ACT.
LOUD MUSIC
DOGS UNLEASHED
NO MAJOR AUTO REPAIR.

PEACE

WELCOME
600 N. TRUMBULL
BLOCK CLUB

NEIGHBORHOOD WATCH IN EFFECT

NO GANG & DRUG
ACTIVITY
CAR WASHING
OR REPAIRING
LOUD MUSIC
LOITERING

HELP KEEP OUR COMMUNITY CLEAN

GHOST HOUSES – Chicago, Ljubljana, Portland, Murcia, Barcelona

These photos document what we call "Ghost Houses." These are remains of a structure that was knocked down long ago. Shadows and outlines of brick, drywall, and concrete linger on neighboring walls. Architectural features like room divisions, closets, painted walls, bits of fixtures and staircases are left behind after the original structure has been torn down. In Chicago these remnants are most often found in poor and blighted sections of the city where rebuilding a home destroyed by fire or neglect may not be an affordable or immediately desirable option. The Chicago photos were taken between 2004 and 2007. The photos from Ljubljana were taken in 2007, and Portland, Oregon and Barcelona and Murcia, Spain in 2008.

Ghost Houses – Ljubljana

BLOCKS OF ICE – Mexico City

During early morning walks along Mexico City streets, it is common to find large blocks of ice sitting, unattended, on the pavement. The blocks vary in size and quantity. They are delivered by pre-arrangement for use by the many vendors who fill the sidewalks and streets selling food and cold beverages (along with countless non-perishable wares). One local explained that in a city where anything that isn't locked down will be stolen, blocks of ice are the one thing people respect and leave alone. These photos were taken in 2007.

Blocks of Ice – Mexico City

WRAPPED VENDOR STALLS – Mumbai

Mumbai is a giant amalgamation of formal and informal activities that symbiotically combine to make the city function. Competition for just about everything is fierce. Many Mumbai residents are self-employed as street vendors. Some have sturdy, well-built, permanent stands that they can lock up at night. Poorer vendors don't have this luxury. They put their goods on blankets or tarps right on the edges of sidewalks. Or, when buildings cover the sidewalks, they place them directly in the street. The smallest of these sidewalk shops consisted of a heavily soiled towel with six "D" batteries for sale. This would be easy for the vendor to pack up and carry home but many of the sidewalk stores have larger inventories. Carrying those on Mumbai's overcrowded buses and trains, where one literally has to push, fight, squeeze, and contort just to get on and off, isn't an option. Remarkably, much of the inventory is wrapped up, often in blue tarps or clear plastic with rope or string, and left on the sidewalk. This has two functions: the vendor doesn't have to carry the material home and it saves his or her spot for the next day. This situation is highly respected and the wrapped vendor stalls are left alone. They are found in all parts of the city, from the desperately poor incremental settlements to the upper class high rise neighborhoods. These photos were taken in 2008.

118 Wrapped Vendor Stalls – Mumbai

MEMORIALS – Fort Wayne, Chicago, Ljubljana

Memorials mark violent, personal tragedies in places not really intended for public expression or mourning. Small crosses – some plain, others adorned with fake flowers, ribbons, photographs, and names – can be seen along highways in the U.S. and other countries. Traffic accidents, drunk driving hit-and-run pedestrian deaths, gang-related shootings, and victims of violent crime are among those commonly memorialized in public. It is generally assumed that the memorial is sited in the place where the death occurred but sometimes a symbolic location is chosen. An example of the latter is an outdoor memorial to a Macedonian pop singer that a record store in Ljubljana created. While probably not legal, we have observed memorials like these that have remained in situ for years in places like Fort Wayne, Indiana, and in Chicago – particularly if they are small and unobtrusive. These photos were taken between 2006 and 2008.

FREE ITEMS – Urbana, Wynnewood

Americans consume more than our fair share of everything from food and energy, to raw materials and processed goods. We gobble up more resources per capita than people in any other part of the world. Most households are filled to overflowing with unneeded or unwanted items; the desire that lead to their purchase has been replaced by the desire to consume something else. Evidence of this destructive abundance can be seen in the rapid growth of the public storage industry in the past five years. People rent extra space to store things that no longer fit in their houses. The excess of American consumption can also be seen on the curbsides of towns like Urbana, Illinois, or Wynnewood, Pennsylvania. People will put a variety of items next to the curb or in front of their house. Anything that people think should be reused, from scraps of wood to exercise machines, are often accompanied by a sign that says "FREE" to make it clear to passersby that the items should be taken. This is an important element in the dialogue about the "sanctity" of private property and who is allowed to enter a property without permission – a taboo in the United States that many from other countries find strange and confusing. Without the sign, it isn't completely clear that one is allowed to enter the private forcefield of the property and take the items. They have an ambiguous status unless the situation is clearly spelled out. If items are on the other side of the sidewalk, and they don't have a sign on them, then it is best to assume that they are not for the taking and the homeowners want to keep the things. The property owners are probably just messy and don't clean up their yards (another taboo in American neighborhoods). These photos were taken in 2007.

134 Free Items - Urbana (top), Wynnewood (bottom)

PILES OF BIKES – Copenhagen

Copenhagen is a bike-friendly city. There are separate lanes for bikes that cars are not allowed to park in, drive through, or otherwise interrupt. Bicyclists have their own traffic signals, which are enforced. This makes it very safe to bike there and many people take advantage of the friendly bicycle climate. They commute to work by bike each day, year-round, regardless of the weather. It is common to find bike stores on nearly every other block in many parts of the city. There is a great deal of surplus money, as well as consumer goods in the wealthy country of Denmark, and this includes bikes. There are many bikes that are abandoned by their owners in public places, or stolen, and left sitting against walls. Bikes are found in piles, all over the city. Some are left at train stations (pages 135 and 136). Authorities identify bikes that have been sitting at train stations for long periods of time. They put orange tags on the bikes to warn the owners of immanent removal. The bikes are then put into piles where they await transport to either the dump or a city auction, depending on their condition. It is also common to see piles of bikes that people no longer want, sitting in the inner courtyards of apartment buildings (top image page 137), or in public parks (bottom image page 137). These photos were taken in 2007.

Piles of Bikes – Copenhagen

Piles of Bikes – Copenhagen 137

WORKSHOP – Ljubljana

In October of 2007, members of Temporary Services led a three-day workshop in Ljubljana, Slovenia organized by Urša Jurman, curator at P74 Center and Gallery. We began by sharing our research with the nine participants. Then everyone explored in Ljubljana. The workshop participants documented public modifications that they found compelling. Each day of the workshop we compared our photographs and tried to make sense of what we found.

The group was filled with hard workers. Over 500 photos were collected in a single weekend. The participants did not limit their documentation to categories that Temporary Services normally looks for, but discovered their own situations to shoot. Together we sorted the photos and the workshop culminated in a public event and slide show at P74 on our last evening in Ljubljana.

While many excellent photos were taken during the workshop, in most cases there were not enough examples to adequately represent new themes for this book. Where possible, we added the participants' photographs to the various categories that we settled on. For this section we invited each participant from the workshop to include a favorite photo from that weekend which was not included elsewhere in this book. Photo credits are listed in the acknowledgments.

RESOURCES

This section gathers together a variety of books, online collections and archives, and artists' projects that document a range of patterns in informal or unofficial uses of city spaces. Some of these efforts have been critical to our work with public phenomena. Other resources emerged or came to our awareness much later and are included to point out a larger conversation that we connect with. Our bias leans toward photographers that show the phenomena they document in context, rather than abstracted or fetishized. When possible, we have tried to review books that were still in print and available at the time of publication.

BOOKS

Bikes of Burden. Kemp, Hans. Hong Kong: Visionary World Ltd., 2003. This book of 150 photos by Hans Kemp documents extraordinary uses of motorbikes on the streets of Vietnam. Metal fencing, dead pigs, dozens of chickens, doors, truck tires and entire families are shown being transported on single bikes. These documents of everyday labor and survival evoke a sense of wonder and complete awe.

Brakin: Brazzaville – Kinshasa. Visualizing the Visible, Edited by Wim Cuyvers, Baden: Lars Müller Publishers and Jan van Eyck Academie, 2006. This book documents the efforts of a group of researchers investigating the interconnectedness of Brazzaville and Kinshasa, separated only by the river Congo. They look for visual evidence in both cities of street children, the architecture of the diamond trade, the United Nations' presence, roundabouts and more. There are plenty of images and maps that show their efforts and attempts to, as they say, "visualize the visible," a convoluted way of saying that they are showing patterns in human behavior and city use.

The Contemporary Picturesque. Norman, Nils. London: Book Works, 2000. In helpfully captioned photos from London, New York, and other cities, this book presents barricades, guardrails, and outdoor seating designed for minimal comfort, anti-sitting and climbing devices and myriad other official models for controlling public behavior. From the other side of the fence, it also documents protest encampments in trees, community gardens and several actions that illegally modified street surfaces.

Edward Fella – Letters On America : photo-graphs and lettering. Fella, Edward. Essays by Lewis Blackwell and Lorraine Wild. New York: Princeton Architectural Press, 2000. Edward Fella is a creator of hand-drawn typography. This book features his own creative work with type but also includes reproductions of over 1,000 Polaroids that he has taken of typography in the world – the kind of anonymous work that is commonly  excluded from graphic design histories. This includes everything from hand drawn advertising text created in marker on poster-board to lettering crafted from broken bits of tile, carved into trees, painted on glass, and stick on type that can be found peeling off of metal surfaces. The book conveys an endless fascination with, and enthusiasm for, lettering in its many public applications.

Endcommercial / Reading the City, Böhm, Florian; Pizzaroni, Luca; and Scheppe, Wolfgang. Ostfildern-Ruit, Germany: Hatje Cantz Publishers, 2002. This book is a must have for people interested in documenting the ways cities change through use by their denizens. It offers a stunning visual adventure through the banalities of city life. It makes the reader excited and inspired by surprising things, like the exhaust vents on the sides of buildings.

Folk Archive: Contemporary Popular Art from the UK, Deller, Jeremy; Kane, Alan. London: Bookworks, 2002. This richly illustrated book attempts to answer the question of, "What might constitute present day folk art?" A vast array of UK-based subjects are considered in full color photos that generally show objects in the contexts that they were created for. Among the subjects: embroidered wrestling costumes, hand-painted food signs, decorated cakes and puddings from a festival in Braithwaite, Cumbria,  sand sculptures, banners at demonstrations, prisoner-designed tattoo guns (identical to ones American prisoners create), signs for clairvoyant hand-reading services, and drawings made with one's finger on the rear doors of a dirty truck. The chief disappointment with this book is that it is only 160 pages and some categories demand a far greater number of photos in order to achieve a more nuanced understanding of their various articulations. Nonetheless, this opens up an expanded view of creativity and its many locations in society.

Graffiti. Brassai, George. Paris: Flammarion Groupe, 2002. Long before there was anything like a graffiti scene with taggers, writers and spray paint, Brassai was roaming the streets of Paris in the 1930s, documenting figures and imagery that he found gauged out of, scrawled, or incised into walls. This book contains many examples of his black and white photos of public markings.

The Historic Centre of Mexico City. Alÿs, Francis detto and Moniváis, Carlos. Spain: Turner Publicaciones, S.L., 2006. This book includes numerous photos taken on the streets of Mexico City. Alÿs' themes include vending culture, homeless encampments, the Zocolo, sleeping people and dogs occupying various public surfaces, blocks of ice sitting on the sidewalk and roving musicians. A text by Carlos Moniváis about Mexico City and Alÿs's documentation runs alongside the images.

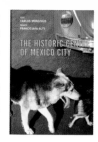

PARK. Stratman, Deborah. Chicago: Temporary Services, 2000. Deborah Stratman researched the architecture of Chicago's parking lot attendant booths while working to make her own portable parking booth. This booklet includes 23 eerie night photos of these minor and easily overlooked one-person buildings. Eight years later, development in the southern part of downtown Chicago is booming and many of these lots no longer exist. They have been sold and the land has been used for constructing large condominiums. Free download: www.temporaryservices.org/PARK.pdf

Sign Language – Street Signs as Folk Art. Baeder, John. New York: Harry N. Abrams, Inc., 1996. A rich photo collection of anonymous professional and amateur hand-painted signage, with some unfortunately patronizing commentary alongside the images. The signs are primarily from the American South and nearly always shown in the context of the buildings, walls, fences or landscapes that they were painted on or affixed to. The illustrations include commercial signage for stores, businesses, services, graffiti (pre-spray-paint tagging), general vandalism, and signs for churches and palm-readers.

WAIT FOR WALK. Böhm, Florian, Essays by Ulrich Pohlmann and Ronald Jones. Germany: Hatje Cantz, 2007. This book focuses on that particular moment, in New York, when people wait at the curb for the traffic signal to change to WALK so that they can cross the street. Böhm's photos show accidental configurations of people from various social strata, each inhabiting the moment of waiting. They stand in rela-

tion to the curb of the street. Many stand behind the curb, as if held back by an invisible fence. Others teeter over the edge or stand in front of the curb as if to carve out a bit more personal space and maintain autonomy from the rest of the group that waits. In her essay, Ulrich Pohlmann compares the sidewalk in these photos to a stage. She also notes that in recent times, because of surveillance and police crackdowns on jaywalking, the photos show the disciplining of public space in New York that has been ramped up since the 1980s more so since 9/11.

ARTISTS' PROJECTS

Many artists have been sources of inspiration for this book. We want to highlight two: Alexis Petroff and Zoe Leonard.

Chicago-based artist Alexis Petroff works in a variety of media including video, gouache and collage. Among his many endeavors, he often returns to documenting several phenomena that interest him. The beautiful handmade accordion-style book *No Rubbish: Scrapper truck photos taken at the Kingsbury Street scrap yard and around town, 1999-2003*, documents trucks in Chicago piled high with recyclable materials. Petroff's photos act as a kind of portraiture by way of truck – which is appropriate given the degree to which many of these vehicles have been customized by their owners so that they can haul off more scraps of metal and metal-laden junk than one might have previously thought possible. Petroff captures the trucks, with their built up sides and caging over the driver's cabins, from the rear as well as in profile. The rear photos emphasize the extraordinary accumulations and organizations of found recyclables. The profile shots allow us to see how the driver has extended the walls of the truck to contain mountains of junk that are pulled from alleys and taken to scrap yards like the large depot at Kingsbury Street.

Despite shifts in format, subject, and approach, Zoe Leonard's photography is consistently socially conscious, deeply poetic, and impeccable in its craft. Her camera has shown us the remains of bear and animal hunting activity in Alaska, the disappearing culture of mom and pop shops in New York City, and the travels of recycled clothing from Brooklyn to Uganda in the globalized rag trade. She has honed in on empty window frames that have been filled in with cinder blocks and painted over – a common sight in New York and many other American cities. We particularly appreciate Leonard's photos beginning in 1998 that show trees in New York escaping their man-made metal boundaries. This book reproduces two variations, both titled *Detail (Tree & Fence)*, which typify the stunning, highly nuanced black and white gelatin silver prints from the series.

Images on the following page:

Top: both are *No Rubbish: Scrapper truck photos taken at the Kingsbury Street scrap yard and around town, 1999-2003*, by Alexis Petroff

Bottom: both are *Detail (Tree & Fence)*, 1998-1999, by Zoe Leonard